Anna

Endless love and thanks to my dear friend Annamaria Gallizio, and her beautiful mother, Renata, and grandmother, Anetta Milos. I would also like to thank Roberto, Mauro and Etcio.

This book would not exist without Masa Sugatsuke, Joyce Lam; Brent Adams and Cassandra Victor of Two Three Two; David Ortega and Laura Genninger of Studio 191 NY; and Jin Lee.

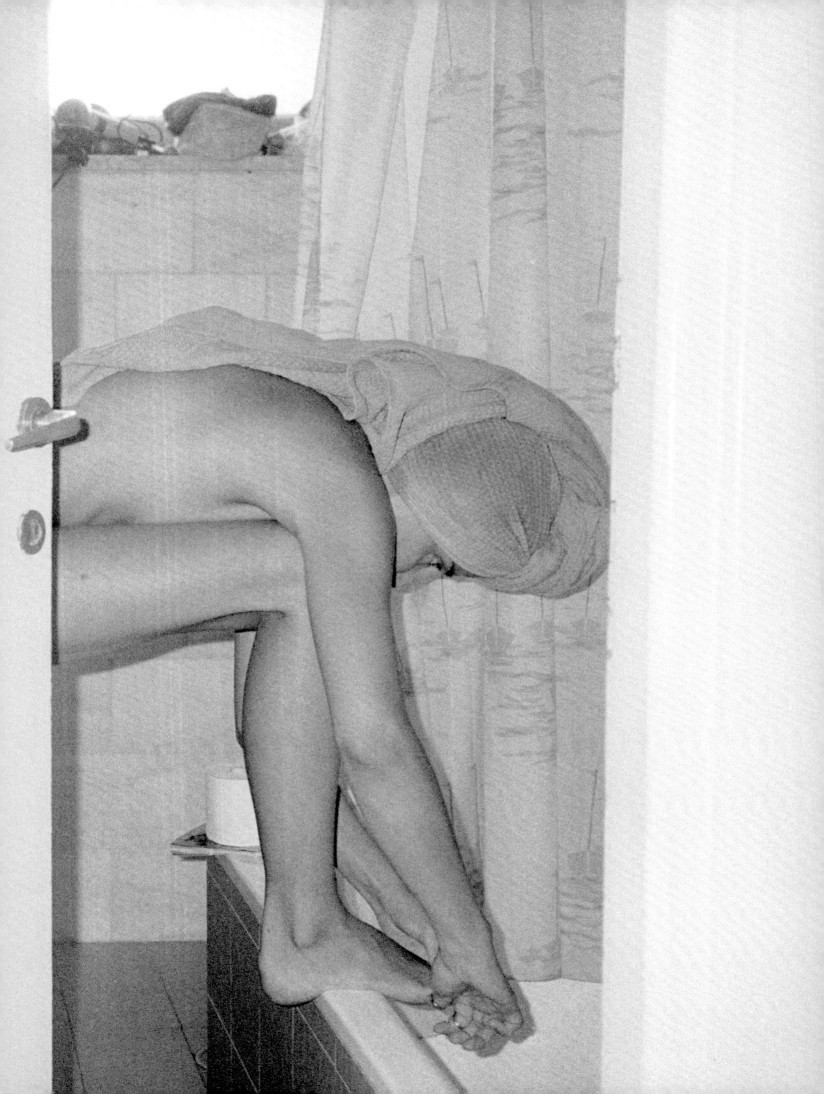

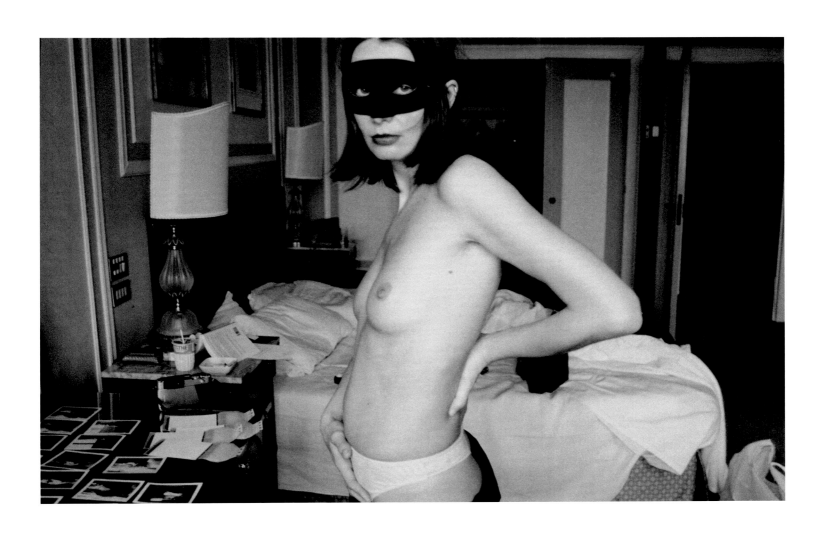

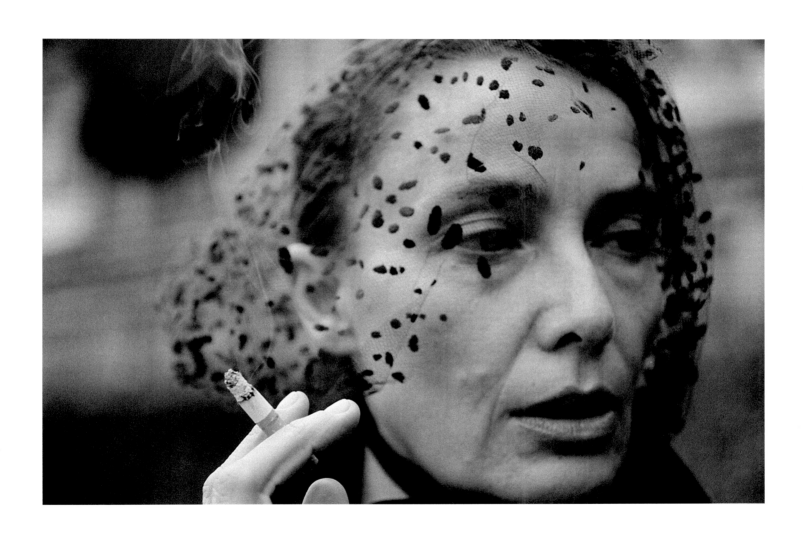

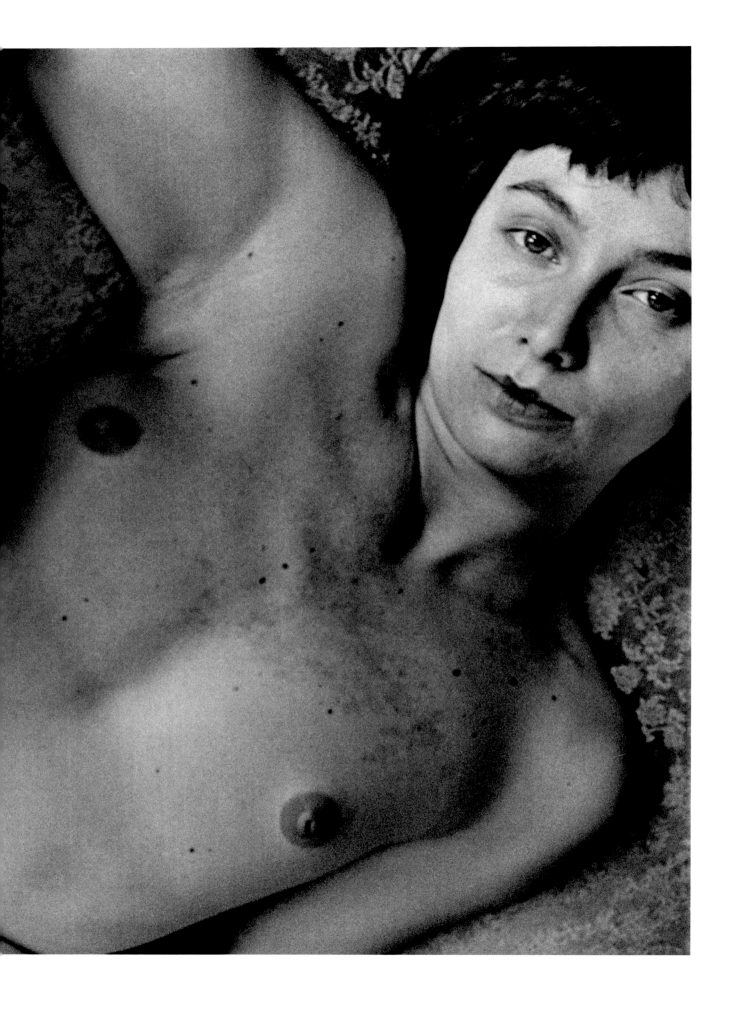

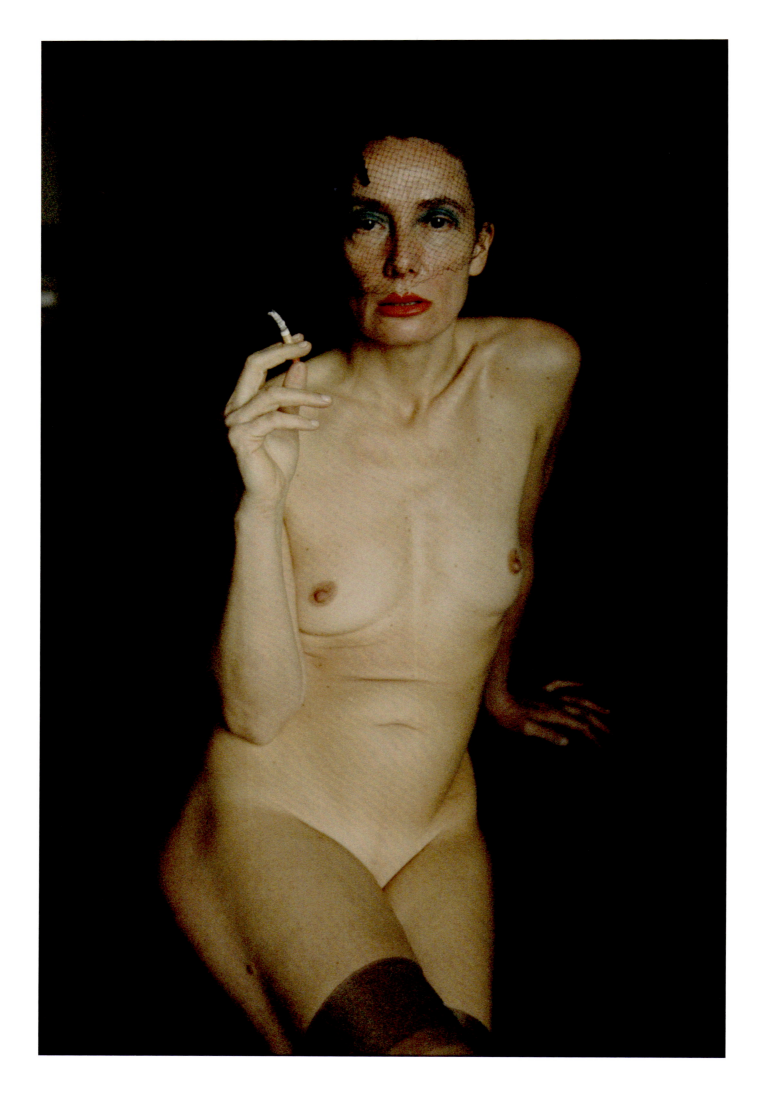

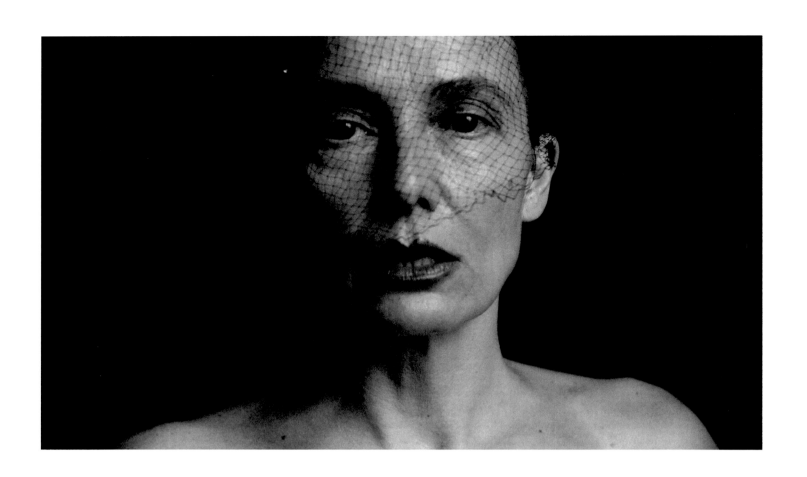

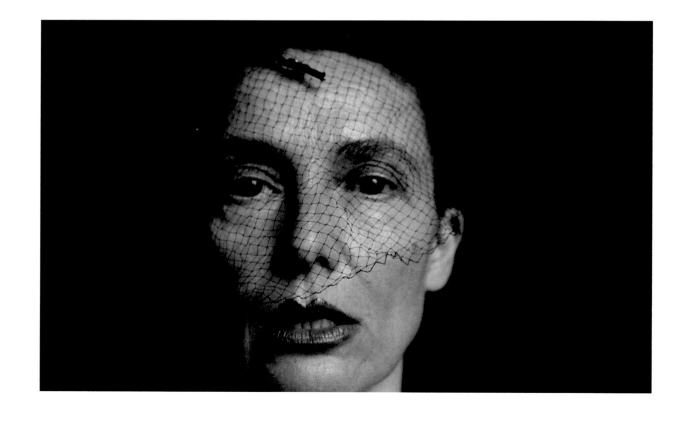

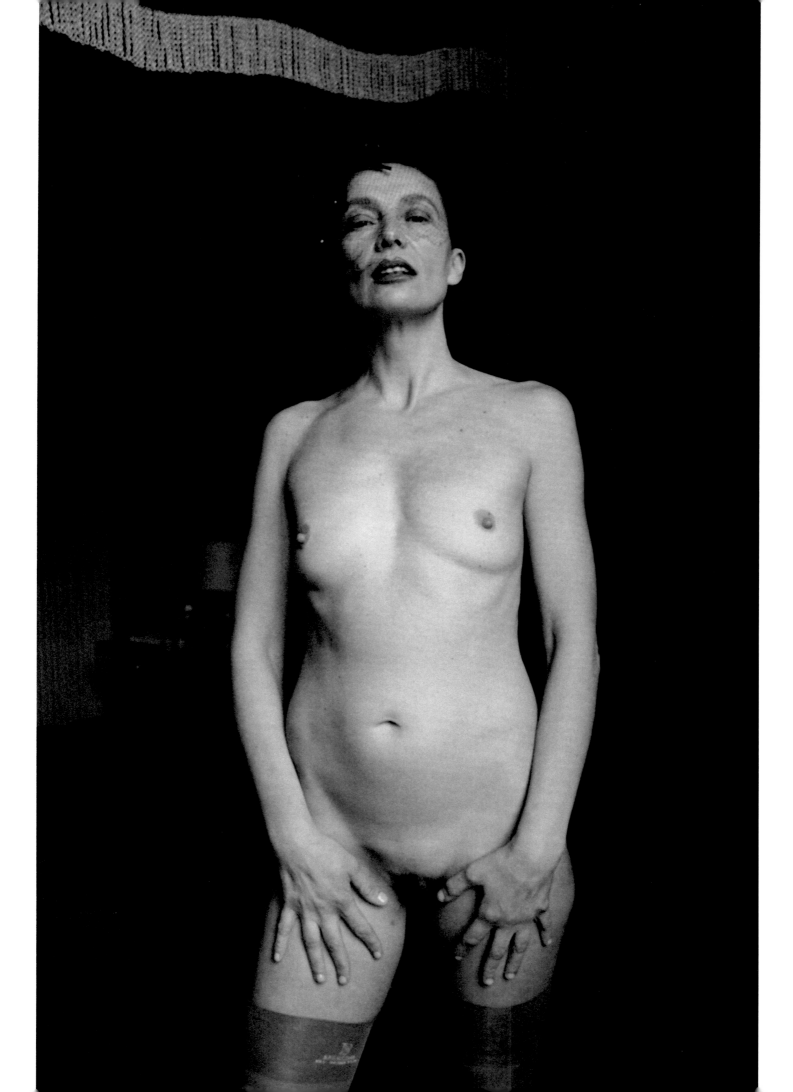

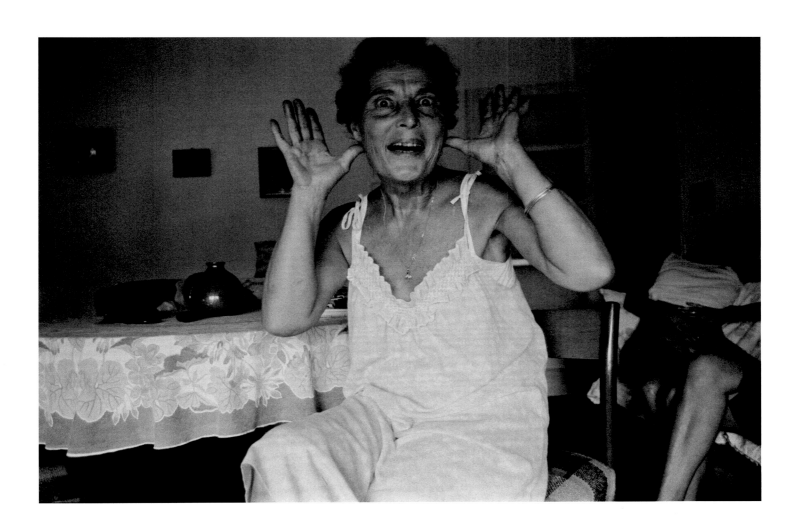

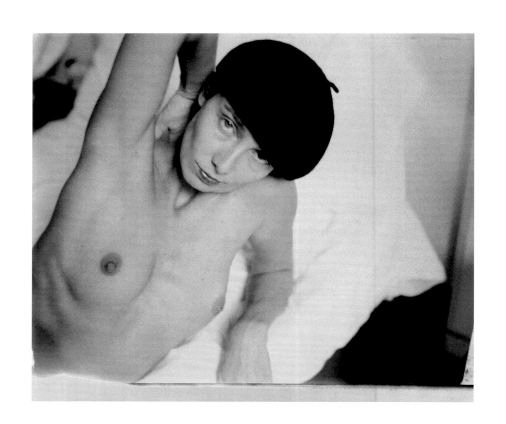

"The tongue can conceal the truth, but the eyes never! You're asked an unexpected question, you don't even flinch, it takes just a second to get yourself under control, you know just what you have to say to hide the truth, and you speak very convincingly, and nothing in your face twitches to give you away. But the truth, alas, has been disturbed by the question, and it rises up from the depths of your soul to flicker in your eyes and all is lost."
- Mikhail Bulgakov, *The Master and Margarita*

Anna

Yelena Yemchuk

ANNA
YELENA YEMCHUK

FIRST EDITION, PUBLISHED IN 2017

EDITOR & PUBLISHER: MASANOBU SUGATSUKE
ASSISTANT EDITOR: JOYCE LAM
ART DIRECTION & BOOK DESIGN: LAURA GENNINGER, DAVID ORTEGA, STUDIO 191 NY
POST PRODUCTION: BRENT ADAMS

PRINTING DIRECTOR: KATSUMI MATSUI, SUNM COLOR CO., LTD.
PRINTING AND BINDING: SUNM COLOR CO., LTD.
THIS MONOGRAPH IS PRINTED IN 1000 DPI.

PUBLISHED BY UNITED VAGABONDS LLC
UNITED VAGABONDS LLC ARE MASAAKI SAKAKIBARA, MASANOBU SUGATSUKE, MISA SHIN, TAKAYUKI ISHII, TONY WONG,
SUNM COLOR CO.,LTD, TOMIO KOYAMA AND YUKO YAMAMOTO.
ADDRESS: 6F, 7-14, NIHONBASHI-YOKOYAMACHO, CHUO-KU, TOKYO JAPAN 103-0003
TEL: 03-3527-3636
INFO@UNITEDVAGABONDS.COM
WWW.UNITEDVAGABONDS.COM

PHOTOGRAPHS © 2017 YELENA YEMCHUK
PUBLICATION © 2017 UNITED VAGABONDS LLC

DISTRIBUTION IN JAPAN: TRANSVIEW
2-30-6 NIHONBASHI-NIGYOCHO, CHUO-KU, TOKYO, JAPAN 103-0013
TEL: 03-3664-7334
WWW.TRANSVIEW.CO.JP

PRINTED IN JAPAN
ISBN 978-4-908600-01-2

All rights reserved. No part of this publication may be reproduced or transmitted in any form or by any means, electronic or mechanical, including photocopy, recording or any other storage and retrieval system, without prior permission in writing from the publisher. All rights reserved. No part of this publication may be reproduced or transmitted in any form or by any means, electronic or mechanical, including photocopy, recording or any other storage and retrieval system, without prior permission in writing from the publisher.

Anna